BLACKBEARD THE PIRATE
AND OTHER STORIES OF
THE PINE BARRENS

New Jersey

Atlantic Ocean

N
W · E
S

1. Where Blackbeard's treasure was buried.
2. Tabernacle
3. Leeds Point
4. Indian Mills
5. Shamong
6. Smithville
7. Philadelphia
8. Greenwich
- - - - Route of the Medicine show
⅄⅄⅄ Pine Barrens

Blackbeard the Pirate and Other Stories of the Pine Barrens

BY LARONA HOMER
Illustrated by William Sauts Bock

THE MIDDLE ATLANTIC PRESS
Wilmington, Delaware

Published by
The Middle Atlantic Press
848 Church Street
Wilmington, Delaware 19899

Manufactured in the United States of America
Composition: Roberts/Churcher, West Chester, PA
Printing and Binding: Fairfield Graphics, Fairfield, PA

ISBN: 0-912608-25-0

Library of Congress Cataloging in Publication Data

Homer, Larona
    Blackbeard the pirate and other stories of the Pine
Barrens.

    Bibliography: p. 96
    SUMMARY: Short stories set in the Pine Barrens of
New Jersey, featuring both real people and legendary
figures who were connected with the area.
    [1. Pine Barrens—Fiction.   2. Short stories]
I. Bock, William Sauts, 1939–   II. Title.
PZ7.H745Bl [Fic]   79-13270
ISBN 0-912608-25-0

For my grandchildren
Jennifer, Susan, Dana, Tacy,
Mark, Deborah, Bruce.
They had many happy times in the Pine Barrens.

Contents

BLACKBEARD THE PIRATE
AND OTHER STORIES OF
THE PINE BARRENS

Jody and the Smithville Silver Cornet Band

More than anything in the world, Jody wanted to lead the Smithville Silver Cornet Band. He went to rehearsals every Monday night in the school auditorium with his father, who played the tuba, and his brother Rick, who played the trumpet. He always brought his ruler with him. Standing in the back of the room, he would wave it in time with the bandmaster's baton, pretending he was the leader.

He knew all the music by heart. He especially liked "The King of Thunder March." But he didn't like the way Mr. Jenkins conducted it. It should sound like a thunderstorm. If he were the bandleader he would start it very softly the way thunder starts to rumble far away. He would have the band get louder and louder as the thunder came closer. Then there would be a long pause. Wasn't it always quiet before the biggest crash of thunder? At the very end the drums and the brass and the cymbals would all burst through together.

One night as they were rehearsing "The King of Thunder March" Jody called out, "More drums!" The drummers must have heard, for they drummed so loudly they almost drowned out the rest of the instruments. Just before they came to the end Jody shouted "Quiet!"

Mr. Jenkins turned around and looked toward

the back of the auditorium. The band members held their instruments in mid-air and they looked too. Jody humped down behind the seats and tried to hide.

"Jody," his father said as they walked home, "you've got to keep quiet if you want to come to rehearsals with us. You must *not* shout out the way you did tonight." By this time his father was shouting too. "And this isn't the first time. You can't tell Mr. Jenkins how to conduct his band. I don't know why he didn't send you home."

"I know, Pa. I didn't mean to do it. It's just that—he doesn't make it sound like thunder. I wish I could lead the band. I'd show them."

"You have to know how to play some of the instruments before you can do that," Rick said.

"Well, when am I going to learn?"

"When you're a little older. There's plenty of time," Pa said. "But I'll speak to H. B. about it sometime."

Hezekiah Bradley Smith, or H. B., as the village people called him, owned the Star Bicycle Factory. He owned the land for miles around it. He owned the big house he called "The Mansion." He owned Jody's house and the houses of all the workers in Smithville. In fact, he owned just about everything in sight, including a moose named February, which he hitched to his carriage and drove through the countryside scaring horses off the roads and into the ditches.

But everyone in Smithville loved H. B. He was a

kind, generous man to work for. He paid good wages. He built a new school for the children and bought new instruments for his band. Every Saturday night the band gave a concert in his bandstand for the villagers.

"Why aren't you in the band?" H. B. asked Jody one Saturday night during intermission.

"I guess I'm not old enough, sir," Jody answered.

"Nonsense. How old are you?"

"Eleven, sir."

"Old enough," said H. B. "Don't you want to play?"

"Oh yes, sir. And someday I'd like to be the band-leader."

"The band-leader, eh? Well, you should learn to play an instrument first. What instrument would you like?"

"A cornet, sir. A shiny silver cornet."

"Humph," said H. B. "We'll have to get you one."

That was weeks ago and Jody didn't hear another word about the cornet. Every day he would practice on Rick's trumpet. He was sure you would play them both the same way.

One Monday night as Jody stood in the back of the auditorium waving his arms pretending he was the leader, H. B. came to rehearsal. As he listened a smile broke out above his chin whiskers. He walked down the aisle clapping his hands and stopped the music.

"I have a great idea," he said. "Next week I'm

going to Washington to see Thomas Finley ride our Star Bicycle down the steps of the Capitol. I want my Smithville Silver Cornet Band to play at the Mt. Holly station when I board the train. You'll all have a holiday."

The band members cheered.

"That's too far for you to walk, so we'll hitch up several farm wagons for you to ride in. You can play along the way," H. B. said.

Everyone was delighted. Everyone except Jody. He couldn't go. He didn't have his cornet.

The big day arrived. The band looked smart in their freshly pressed blue uniforms. Their brass buttons shone and their instruments gleamed in the morning sun. Everyone in the village turned out to wave goodbye to Hezekiah Bradley Smith and to wish him well.

Just as his moose February was about to pull the carriage away, H. B. spotted Jody and called, "Say there Jody, why aren't you playing in the band?"

But February had started and the Smithville Silver Cornet Band was tooting so loudly that H. B. couldn't hear Jody answer, "I don't have anything to play."

It was a bad day for Jody. He was disappointed and cross. Disappointed because he had to stay in stupid old Smithville while Rick had a holiday in Mt. Holly. And cross because H. B. had promised him a cornet and hadn't gotten it for him.

"Why do grown-ups make promises if they don't keep them?" Jody said aloud. Then he kicked some stones down the path that turned into the woods. There he could at least chase squirrels and think.

After H. B.'s successful return from Washington, everything in Smithville was quiet for a while. Orders for the Star Bicycle kept coming in. The Smithville Silver Cornet Band kept rehearsing. Jody kept waiting for his cornet and going to rehearsals and conducting in the back of the auditorium where Mr. Jenkins couldn't see him.

A few weeks later, H. B. came to rehearsal again. Two tailors were with him. He clapped his hands. The band stopped playing.

"My Friends and Musicians," he said, "I have decided to run for United States Congress."

The band members looked at one another and whispered their surprise. Mr. Jenkins tapped his music stand to get order.

"Yes," said H. B. "I'm going to start my campaign in a few weeks right here in Burlington County. Then I'll go all over the state. And you are going to accompany me with your music. My Smithville Silver Cornet Band will play everywhere I stop to make a speech."

Cheers broke out. This would be much more exciting than the trip to Mt. Holly.

"And you will all have new uniforms for the campaign. I think they should be red—with gold braid—and gold stripes down the trouser legs. How would you like that?"

"Yes, yes," they all shouted.

Mr. Jenkins tapped his music stand again for quiet.

"We'll start right now to measure you. If you'll put your instruments aside and form a line here my tailors will begin with the trumpets and cornets."

The two men came to the front of the auditorium with their tape measures, pads and pencils and started to measure each band member.

"And now, my Friends and Musicians, I'll leave you to finish your rehearsal. Do well. Not every future congressman will have a silver cornet band to play for him."

As H. B. started up the aisle he noticed Jody sitting quietly in the back.

"Well, Boy, why aren't you playing with the band?" he asked.

"I don't have any instrument, sir," Jody said.

"No instrument? We ordered a cornet for you from Boston. Hasn't it come yet?"

"I guess not, sir."

"We'll have to see about that. You better go up and be measured—in case it's here in time," and H. B. clapped his hands again and called to one of the tailors. "Measure Jody too. He's going to be a member of the band."

Jody was so excited he had trouble falling asleep that night. When he finally did drop off he dreamt that he was in his new red uniform with its gold braid and brass buttons playing his shiny new cornet. Then his dream changed and he was standing on a platform leading the band. He could hear the drums get louder and louder and at the end he brought in the cymbals and all the brass with a deafening crash. Everyone applauded. He bowed, first to the right, then to the left, then to the center. H. B. smiled at him from the audience, then came up and shook his hand.

But it wasn't really H. B. shaking him. It was his mother trying to waken him for school.

It was difficult for Jody to keep his mind on lessons the next few days. Each afternoon he would hurry to the post office to see if the cornet had arrived. Three weeks went by.

The next Monday night H. B. came to rehearsal with the two tailors. They had the new uniforms to be tried on. Jody's fit perfectly.

"It'll be a shame if your cornet doesn't come," the trombone player said. "After all, you can't be in the band if you don't have an instrument, can you?"

Jody bit his lip hard. "Maybe it'll come tomorrow," he said.

But it didn't come the next day. Nor the next. Nor the next. And the following day they were to start H. B.'s campaign.

It was a very sad Jody who climbed into bed that last night. Before he went to sleep his father came in and sat on the edge of the bed.

"I'm sorry, Jody," he said, "but there will be more times coming along. You'll be able to play in the bandstand concerts when your cornet arrives."

"*If* it arrives," Jody said and turned his face to the wall so Pa couldn't see his tears.

Early the next morning Jody sat at the breakfast table watching his mother as she helped Pa and Rick into their new uniforms. His untouched bowl of cereal was cold in front of him. He was feeling so sorry for himself he didn't pay attention to the knock at the kitchen door. Pa opened it. There stood H. B.—his high silk hat pushed to the back of his head—his red silk bow tie slightly askew under his chin whiskers. He pushed right past Pa and started over to Jody waving his gold-headed cane.

"Get into your uniform, Boy," he said. "You've got to lead the band. Mr. Jenkins fell and broke his leg. I've watched you at rehearsals in the back of the auditorium. Why, you know the music as well as he does. Come on Jody, *move*." And like a gust of wind, H. B. blew out of the house.

Jody was too surprised to say anything. Pa helped him out of his nightshirt. His mother helped him into his uniform. Rick buttoned the brass buttons—all in a matter of minutes.

They hurried down to the school. The members of the Smithville Silver Cornet Band were standing in formation on the school steps holding their instruments. The villagers had gathered there to see them off. Three large farm wagons decorated with red, white and blue bunting were close by, ready to carry the band from town to town. H. B. was sitting in his brand new carriage holding his gold-headed cane. February was pawing at the ground anxious to start.

H. B. called Jody over to his carriage and handed him a new baton with a real silver tip. "Let's hear 'The King of Thunder March,' before we start," he said.

"*Yes sir!*" Jody said. He jumped up on the large box that someone had placed on the steps in front of the band. Someone else put a music stand on it. Jody rapped on the stand with his baton for attention. They began playing very softly at first, keeping perfect time with Jody's baton.

"Come on now," he whispered, urging them to play louder.

And louder they played. It sounded just the way thunder sounds as it rolls closer and closer. Before the very end, Jody held his arms still. His baton didn't move one little bit. There wasn't a note from the band until he waved his baton again bringing the drums and the brass and the cymbals all crashing in at the same time.

The crowd cheered. Jody turned and bowed. H. B. beamed and applauded. Then he stood up in his carriage and shouted, "Good Boy, Jody. Now let's be off."

The musicians climbed into the farm wagons holding their instruments under their arms. H. B. nodded to his driver and February started the procession, followed by the happy members of the Smithville Silver Cornet Band riding in red-white-and-blue-bedecked wagons. But the happiest member of the whole procession was Jody. He carried something much more important than an instrument. He carried a baton which meant that he was the leader of the band.

The Traveling Medicine Show

Pa had painted the wooden wagon with wide red and white stripes. Through the center stripe on each side he had printed in large black letters, DR. JOHN'S CURE-ALL.

Keziah stood off looking at it. "Pa, you don't have the letters in the center," she said. "They start too near the front on one side, and too near the back on the other side."

Pa walked around the wagon inspecting the printing. Then he walked around it again.

"You're right," he said, putting his arm across the little girl's shoulder. "You're sure right. But we can fix that." And he painted a big yellow sun with a smiling face at each end where the lettering stopped.

Now they were bumping through the Pines in their red-and-white-striped wagon. The April rains had made ruts in the sandy roads, and as they bounced over them everything inside the wagon rattled. The pots and pans clattered against one another on their wall hooks. Pa's medicine bottles that lined one whole side would have jiggled right off their shelves if he hadn't nailed a wooden rail across to hold them in place. Even the sheets and blankets that Keziah folded so neatly every morning and stacked in the corner had tumbled off the pile.

Keziah frowned. She wished they weren't always on their way somewhere. If only they would stop some place long enough for her to make just *one* friend.

She looked in the tiny mirror hanging from a hook in the shelf.

Her pigtails needed brushing. She hated to un-plait and brush and braid them again. Pa had tried to do it many times, but he didn't have much patience. He pulled, and sometimes tears came to her eyes. He didn't mean to hurt. Ma had always said he was very gentle. He was, too. He'd try to comfort her when the kids called her "carrot top," or "freckles," or "skinny." This happened in some of the villages where they stopped with their medicine show.

"But they won't say that any more, now that you have your new green dancing dress," Pa had said. "They'll see how pretty you are."

"No, Pa." Keziah had answered. "I'm not pretty."

She hated the green eyes that looked back at her from the mirror. She hated her red hair. She hated her freckles. She hated living in the gaudy old wagon with DR. JOHN'S CURE-ALL painted on the sides. She hated Pa's calling it his medicine shop, because people in the villages knew it was really just a peddler's wagon. She hated filling all those bottles from the large glass jars with the sticky compounds Pa made from his roots and herbs. She hated to sing and jig for people while Pa sold his Cure-All.

She thought of the time when they had lived in a

house—before Ma went to heaven. Often then Pa would play his mouth organ or fiddle and Ma would sing in her beautiful clear voice, "Little Firefly, Light My Way Home Tonight."

Now DR. JOHN'S CURE-ALL wagon was the only home they had. She and Pa spent all their time traveling with his medicines, "down south" in the winter time, "up north" in the summer. Keziah thought that sometime she'd run away. She could even do it tonight. Somebody in the village would surely take her in. Pa didn't need her to sell his old medicines. He could take her dancing dress back to the store where he had bought it. She felt much more comfortable in her faded overalls anyway.

Pa called to her from the driver's seat, "We're almost to Lower Bank, Keziah. Dolly seems to know she'll soon be unhitched. I don't even have to guide her."

Keziah knew what this meant.

"All right, Pa. I'll get things ready for lunch."

Pa drove the wagon to an open space under some tall pine trees. A clear stream ran not far away. He jumped down from his seat and un-hitched the horse, patting her on the flanks. "Now Dolly, see if you can find something to eat here in this sand," he said.

Keziah pulled aside the canvas curtains at the back of the wagon, lowered the tailboard and jumped out. Then she reached for the basket of food.

"It's going to be a good lunch today, Pa," she said. A lady on the road from Herman had packed it as payment for the medicine Pa had sold her.

"Look Pa, fried chicken, fresh baked bread, cheese and two big red apples."

"Well Keziah, we won't be able to dawdle over it. We've a half hour's drive to Lower Bank yet, and business is best there right after lunch."

"But Pa, this is the best meal we've had in weeks," Keziah said. "Don't let's hurry. Let's make it last."

"Oh Ziah," he sighed, "sometimes I think this is a pretty mean life for a young lady."

"I'm not a young lady. I'm only eleven and I don't want to be a lady. Oh Pa, I wish I was a boy."

"There, there," her father said, putting his arm around her thin shoulders. The sun filtered through the trees, falling on Keziah's red hair. It looked like flames in the bonfire they sometimes had when they slept out under the trees at night. Keziah liked those nights much better than sleeping in the wagon. There the quarters were awfully cramped.

"You'll get all dressed up in your green dancing dress and you'll look so pretty. And all our patients will love to hear you sing and see you jig."

"Oh Pa," she cried, bursting into tears, "I don't want to get dressed up and I won't look pretty with this awful red hair and I'm tired of singing and jigging. And I hate this old show. I wish we had a home to go to at night like the kids in the villages—where we could sleep in a bed, and I could have a puppy and go to school."

"Ziah," he said, smoothing her red hair, "I think you're the prettiest girl a father ever had. And you just wait till we've sold some more medicine. Then maybe we can buy a little house somewhere around here, and you can have a puppy and go to school." He wiped her tears away and held her close for a minute. "Now let's see how good this chicken is. Do you have a smile for your Pa?"

Keziah tried to smile. Pa had said this so many times. But she was sure they would always live in DR. JOHN'S CURE-ALL wagon.

"Now Ziah, we've got to get moving," Pa said as they finished their lunch. "You clear away and I'll take care of Dolly."

Keziah washed the dishes in the stream, put them in the basket and climbed back in the wagon. Pa hitched up the horse and they were off again.

"Better get into your dancing dress," he called from the front.

Keziah took off the faded blue overalls and put on the green dress. But she didn't swirl around to see how it flared out. She didn't even look in the mirror as she tied the bright green ribbons around her pigtails.

It was just after one o'clock when they drove into Lower Bank. They headed right for the open space between the General Store and the Post Office. Pa again unhitched Dolly and wrapped the reins around a post. He worked fast, pulling aside the curtains and lowering a pair of steps attached to the back of the wagon.

He stepped out on the top step, took a mouth organ from his pocket and began to play a lively little tune. A few men and some children came over to see what was going on. Pa stopped his music. In a booming voice he said, "Ladies and Gentlemen, gather round here. Dr. John has once more come to Lower Bank with his famous medicines—guaranteed to cure whatever ails you. Step right up and buy a bottle."

The townspeople began to gather.

"Now Ladies and Gentlemen," he said putting his mouth organ in his pocket, "let me tell you about this new discovery I have. I can't tell you the secret formula, but I guarantee it will ease those aches and pains everywhere from your big toe to the top of your head. Keziah, bring me a bottle."

Keziah stepped out from behind the canvas curtain in her green dancing dress. It seemed to match the color of her eyes.

"What a pretty child," she heard a lady near the front say.

She handed Pa a large bottle.

"Come now," Pa said. "Anybody with an ache or pain needs this bottle of Dr. John's Cure-All."

He'd sold several bottles when someone shouted, "Play us another tune."

He reached in the wagon, brought out his fiddle and began to play. Then just as quickly as he had reached for the fiddle he put it away and held up another bottle of Cure-All.

"Now folks, who needs my medicine?"

"I'll take a bottle," someone in the back of the crowd called.

"So will I," said another person.

For the next few minutes men and women pushed through to buy the secret formula.

When the rush was over for a few minutes Pa said, "Maybe you're ready for the big treat we have for you today. A very beautiful young lady is going to render some very nice songs for you." He took Keziah's hand and helped her out on the steps beside him. In a clear sweet voice she started to sing, "Dear Little Firefly Light My Way Home Tonight."

Applause broke out when she was finished.

"More!" shouted the crowd.

By now almost everyone in town was gathered around the wagon.

"You'll have more just as soon as I've taken care of the patients who need my Cure-All."

Men and women held up their hands, anxious to buy. Keziah went back into the wagon, and as fast as she could take the bottles off the shelves and hand them to Pa, they were sold. Some men opened their bottles right there to take a dose, declaring they felt better immediately.

"Well now, would you like my little girl to sing another number?"

"Yes!" they shouted.

This time Keziah sang about a little lost dog,

ending, "If you find my little yellow dog, won't you please send him home to me."

It was a sad little story, and the way Keziah sang it brought handkerchiefs from many pockets to wipe away tears.

Pa played his fiddle again ending with a good lively tune. Keziah danced a jig to it, her toes tap-tap-tapping on the wooden steps in front of the wagon's tailboard. Her green skirt swirled high, showing all the ruffles on her pretty pink petticoat. Her pigtails with the bright green bows were flying in time with her toes.

When she finished the crowd clapped and clapped. She sang more songs and danced more jigs, and in between Pa kept selling his Cure-All.

At last when she seemed to have no breath left she sat down on the top step. Pa put his fiddle away. Then he leaned down, patted her head and whispered, "My, you look pretty."

Pa turned back to the crowd. "Anyone else want an extra bottle to put on your shelf at home? We won't be back for a long time."

By now everyone in town seemed to have the Cure-All.

"Well folks," Pa said, "Keziah and I have to be on our way. But we'll see you next year and Keziah will have some new songs to sing for you."

There was more applause and the crowd started to leave. Pa pulled up the steps and closed the canvas curtain. He looked with satisfaction at the bare medicine shelves. As he climbed to the front of the wagon he said, "We'll have to mix up a bigger batch next time." He hitched up Dolly and once more they were on their way.

Keziah looked at herself in the mirror on the empty shelf. Her hair *was* kind of pretty with the green bows. She *did* like her dancing dress with its wide skirt and pink ruffled petticoat. It felt good to wear it instead of those faded overalls. The freckles on her nose didn't stand out so plain. The people liked her songs, particularly the one about the little yellow dog. And they liked her jigs. They even seemed to feel better after they took Pa's medicine.

She really could never run away from Pa. He needed her. And besides, it wasn't so bad in DR. JOHN'S CURE-ALL wagon. She had a chance to travel all through the countryside and see places that many of the Pineys didn't even know were there. Perhaps tonight she and Pa would have a bonfire and sleep out under the stars.

The Prince of the Pine Barrens

Prince Constantino pushed his cap to the back of his head as he waited at the gate for his Indian friend. The morning sun was slanting through the trees. Little Bear had said he would come when the sun reached the middle branch of the old pine. It was almost there when Constantino heard a low whistle, "Whip-wee-weer, whip-wee-weer." It was their secret call. He whistled back, "Whip-wee-weer, whip-wee-weer." The two boys ran toward each other laughing.

"What are we going to do today?" Constantino asked.

"Want to see where the beaver is building his dam?"

"Sure. Where is it?"

"Down by the pond," Little Bear said.

He took a yellow headband from his pocket and tied it around his shiny black hair to keep it out of his eyes. The hunting knife his grandfather had given him was tucked in his belt.

"Indian braves should carry a hunting knife," the old grandfather had told Little Bear. "Often you need it—like a good friend."

He and Constantino had used it to clear their path in the woods when they got in a tangle of vines. They might need it today. The bushes were thick around the beaver pond.

"You ready?" the Indian boy asked.

"I want to go in the house first," Constantino said."I want you to see the turtle I found after you went home yesterday. I don't know what kind it is."

Little Bear liked the big house that Constantino lived in. The thick carpets felt so soft on his bare feet. It was fun to slide down the banister and make faces at himself in the huge mirrors. Constantino's father called the house a *palazzina*.

"That's what they would call it in Italy where my papa was born," the little prince said. Papa tells me stories about his country across the Atlantic Ocean. He said I should call you 'Amico.'"

"But my name is Little Bear."

"But 'amico' means friend in my papa's language."

Little Bear thought a minute. "Amico," he said. "I like that. Yes, you call me 'Amico.' And I will call *you* 'Amico,' for you are *my* friend."

The two amicos went through the mama's garden where roses and lilies and petunias were blooming. These weren't the kinds of flowers that grew in Little Bear's woods.

"Is your mama here now?"

"No. She and my papa have gone to Washington to see your President Harrison. But they're coming home tonight."

The boys ran up the wide front steps and through the heavy door with its shiny brass knocker, into the house. Little Bear had told his mother about the house where his friend lived with his beautiful mama and his handsome papa, Prince Ruspoli, who was from a royal family.

The mama wore silk dresses that made a sound when she walked, like the rustling of leaves when the wind blew through the trees. And she wore beads around her neck. Not the kinds the Indians wore. Hers sparkled the way dew drops sparkle in the early morning sun. The papa had a large gold watch. He kept it in his pocket on a chain. Even Constantino wore a gold ring on his finger.

Little Bear told his mother that this house had so many rooms that sometimes when he and Constantino would hide they couldn't find each other. He told her about the beautiful red curtains that hung from ceiling to floor on each side of the tall windows. And about the mirrors that were big enough to reflect the whole room—the same way Lake Shamong could reflect the stars in the sky at night.

The handsome papa had come here to help Italy and the United States to be better friends. They called him an ambassador. When he first visited the Pine Barrens he liked it so much he built the *palazzina* for his wife.

"And I was born right here," Constantino said. "Almost the same place you were born."

"We're both ten years old, so it was almost the same time, too," Little Bear said. "Instead of 'Amico,' we should call each other, 'Twin Brother.'" The two boys laughed.

"I don't know the word for 'twin brother,' but

we'll always be good friends, won't we?"

"Always," said Little Bear.

They ran up to Constantino's bedroom to get the turtle. It was in a large basket filled with grass. Little Bear pushed the grass aside.

"It's a painted turtle," he said. "Many of them are here in the Pine Barrens. But he doesn't want to live in a basket. I think you should set him free."

"I will. I just wanted you to see him first." They took him to the garden and put him under the roses.

As they started down the path to the woods someone called from the house, "Don't stay too long."

"Who was that?" Little Bear asked.

"That was cook. She's always afraid something bad will happen to me."

"Here in these woods!" said Little Bear. "What could happen to you here?"

"I don't know. I might get lost, I guess."

"Oh no, you won't get lost. We'll watch the way the sun travels in the sky. The beaver pond is west. That's the way the sun is going. And watch for moss. It grows on the north side of the trees. You can always tell your direction. When we've come to the three fallen trees we're almost there."

"Little Bear, you know so much about the woods."

The Indian boy looked into the brown eyes of the prince. "My father and grandfather are the ones who know about the woods. They show me these things and say, 'We want you to remember all of this. Some day the Indians won't live this way. They'll live the way the white man lives. They'll work in factories the way the white man works. They won't know about the forest and the little beaver and the deer and other animals and birds that live here.'"

"Why do they say that?" Constantino asked.

"My grandfather tells me that since the white man has come here many of our tribe have left and gone to far away places to live."

"Just the way my papa left Italy," Constantino said.

"Oh no," said Little Bear. "If your papa went back to Italy he'd live the same way he always did—in the same kind of big house. My people left because the white man moved in and changed everything. He took our land away from us. Now the Indians have no home to come back to."

They walked on for a while without talking. The prince thought how unfair it was for the white man to make the Indians move from the land where Little Bear's father and grandfather had lived so long.

They came to the three dead trees and climbed over them.

"We're almost there now," Little Bear said.

The path turned again and opened up on a stream of brown cedar water. "Here he comes now," whispered the Indian boy.

The beaver was swimming upstream with a long, slender sapling held tightly in his mouth.

"He's going to wedge that into the dam he's building," Little Bear said.

Just then one end of the sapling caught in a tangle of bushes growing along the edge of the water. The beaver tugged to free it. The sapling wouldn't budge. He tugged again. The bushes held tight. Then he let go, nosed under the sapling and pushed it downstream. It swung loose from the bank. Diving under it, the beaver again grasped it in his mouth and swam to the dam, anchoring it in place.

The boys laughed. He looked so funny. "He wouldn't let those bushes steal his sapling from him," Little Bear said.

All afternoon they tramped through the woods. They watched the red squirrels chase each other. They listened to birds call across the forest. They ate wild huckleberries. They lay under the pines on the soft needles that had dropped there for dozens of years, and just talked.

The sun was shining on the opposite side of the forest.

"I guess we better go home. The cook will be sure I'm lost this time," the prince said.

As they got near the *palazzina* they heard his father calling, "Constantino, Constantino."

"They're home from Washington!" the boy said. Then he called, "Here we are. We're coming," and he ran to meet his father.

Prince Ruspoli leaned over and hugged his son. "Where have you two woodsmen been today?" he asked.

Constantino began to tell all they had seen and done. He laughed again as he told how the beaver wouldn't let the sapling get away from him.

Little Bear stood quietly by, his black eyes dancing at the thought of the good day they'd had.

"That beaver sounds like a smart fellow," the papa said. "I'd like to see him."

"Papa, if you would come to the dam with us tomorrow, maybe you will."

Prince Ruspoli shook his head and frowned. "Constantino, I must tell you something very sad. I'm glad Little Bear is with you to hear what I say.

"President Harrison has just given me orders from Italy to come back home. Our work here is finished. We have made good friends with the American people, and now we must leave."

"Papa, do you mean I will have to leave my good amico? That I'll never see Little Bear again?"

"Yes son, I'm afraid it must be that way. But you will always remember him and the good times you had together."

"No, no, Papa. I won't go! I'll stay here and live with Little Bear."

"You can't do that," his father said putting his arm around the boy's shoulder. "What would your mother and I do without you? We came here because we had work to do. We had to make a strong bond between our two countries. Now they are good friends, just as you and Little Bear are good friends. We will go home to Italy until we get orders to leave for another country. That is the work of an ambassador."

He put his hand on the Indian boy's shiny black hair. "You are an ambassador too, Little Bear," he said. "Ever since Constantino met you down by the lake you have been showing him the ways of the woods. You have taught him to love the trees and the little animals and birds that live here. He has learned much from you. Yes, you are a good ambassador."

The little prince was trying hard to hold back his tears. It didn't seem fair that he wouldn't see Little Bear any more. Then he looked at his gold ring. "Papa, may I give this to Little Bear?"

His father nodded.

He put the ring in Little Bear's hand. "Here, keep this. You are my best friend."

Little Bear slipped the ring on the middle finger of his brown hand. He wished he had something to give Constantino.

Then he thought of his knife. He took it from his belt. "My grandfather said that often you need a hunting knife—like a good friend," and he handed it to the little prince. "Goodbye, Amico." He turned and without looking back, he walked down the path and disappeared in the forest.

Black Doctor of the Pines: James Still

Tim opened his eyes. It was nearly dark. Or was it nearly light? The glow of the oil lamp cast a tall shadow of the ladder-back chair on the opposite wall. As Tim watched the shadow flicker he could make out the large red roses in the wallpaper. This wasn't his room. This was the guest room next to his parents' bedroom. His eyes traveled to the open window where a warm breeze blew through the lace curtains. Then he turned his head to the side. Someone was sitting in the chair beside the bed. It wasn't Father. It wasn't Mother. Tim squinted to see better.

"Good morning, Tim," rumbled a big deep voice—but the kindest voice in the world. "How do you feel now?"

Tim looked into the eyes of the large black man sitting there so quietly. Even in the dim light he could tell he was smiling. Tim knew who it was.

"Good morning, Dr. Still. I'm hungry."

"Well that's the best news yet." Dr. Still stood up. He was taller than the shadow of the chair on the opposite wall. He put his big cool hand on Tim's forehead. Then he felt his cheek. "It's a good sign when a boy is hungry," he said. "That means he's getting better." Taking a large gold watch from his pocket he pressed the stem and opened the case. "It's almost breakfast time. The sun will be shining in your window soon and you're going to feel really good after you've had something to eat. I hear your mother stirring. I'll go and see her."

Dr. Still turned down the wick in the oil lamp until the flame went out. He smoothed Tim's pillow and covers. "I'll be back around noon," he said and quietly left the room.

In the hall Tim could hear the doctor talking to his mother. "His fever is gone. There's no doubt about it now, he's going to be just fine, but he'll need several days in bed. Keep giving him my herb medicine. I'll look in on him later."

Then Tim heard the clop, clop, clop of Dr. Still's horse and the wheels of his little black carriage start down their drive.

Mother was smiling when she came into the room.

"Good morning, Tim. I'm so glad you're feeling better. You gave us quite a scare. But Dr. Still says that by the time your father is home next week you'll be just fine."

"How long was Dr. Still here?" Tim asked.

"He sat by your side all night long. He sent me to bed to get some rest.

"Dr. Still is a good doctor, isn't he?"

"He's a very good doctor, and he's a great man," said Mother.

"I wonder why he stayed here all night," Tim said, more to himself than to his mother.

"Because, Tim," Mother said, "he wanted to be sure you were going to get well. Dr. Still is concerned about all his patients, but most of all about children. I suppose one reason is because he had such a hard life when he was your age."

"How do you mean?" Tim asked.

"When he was only nine—two years younger than you are—he had to chop wood for people in town, or collect rails in the cedar swamps, or help his father make charcoal, which they sold to factories. He had many little brothers and sisters and his father needed all the money James could earn. In the summer he had to pick huckleberries for the farmers in the area. In the autumn he picked cranberries. Then in winter it was back to chopping wood again."

"Didn't he go to school?" Tim asked.

"No. There wasn't time for that. Besides, it's hard to try to study when you're cold and hungry. Often he didn't have proper clothing to keep him warm, and many days there wasn't enough food to eat."

"Why didn't someone help him?" Tim was puzzled. "Why didn't his father get a good job and earn money?"

"Timmy, it's hard to understand," his mother said, "but a black man wasn't allowed to earn a living the way a white man was. His father and mother had been slaves in Maryland. His father had worked hard there in the fields. He bought his freedom. Then he brought his wife and two little girls to New Jersey. Here James was born. But his father had spent all his money to buy his freedom.

They had nothing left when they got here."

"Where did they live?" Tim's brown eyes were wide with concern.

"They moved in with an old black man named Cato, who had a tiny little house in Indian Mills. After many months Mr. Still got work in the saw-mill there. It didn't pay very much. It was hard for all of them. Cato's house was so small. It had only one door and no windows. The fireplace gave the only heat in the house, and there weren't any carpets on the cold dirt floor. And the Still family was growing larger each year."

Sam, Tim's big gray cat, jumped up on the bed. He snuggled up beside Tim.

"Golly, Sam," Tim said scratching his ears, "we have it easy. I'm glad I don't have to cut wood all winter and pick berries all summer." Then after a long pause he asked, "How did Dr. Still ever become a doctor?"

Mother thought a minute. "He told me that, when he was a very little boy, a Dr. Fort came to the Pine Barrens to vaccinate the children. James was most interested in the way he cleaned his arm with alcohol, scratched it and used the vaccine. Dr. Fort explained all he was doing. He told James that this would prevent children from getting smallpox—that horrible sickness that everyone feared. James decided right then that he wanted to be a doctor and help people the way Dr. Fort did. He never changed his mind, but as he got older he knew this would be difficult because he would

have to have an education. He didn't know just how it would happen, but someday he would help sick people to become well."

"But how *did* he do it?" Tim asked, propping himself up on his elbow and putting his head in his hand.

Just then the clock in the hall struck eight.

"My goodness, Tim. I must get your breakfast. Dr. Still said you should begin to eat," Mother said. "I'll finish the story when I bring in your tray."

As she went downstairs Tim closed his eyes and tried to imagine his family living in a little log cabin with no windows. And there were only three of them—plus Sam. He thought of the cozy nights he and Mother and Father spent sitting in their warm living room reading or telling stories. The Still family must have had to sit awfully close to the fireplace. Even then only one side of you would be warm. And just a cold dirt floor with no rugs! Tim was glad he didn't have to get up every winter morning and go out chopping wood without enough clothing to keep out the cold—and hungry besides.

He was hungry now, and it wasn't funny. But he knew Mother would be here any minute with apple juice and hot oatmeal with cream on it.

Sam stretched out beside him, then curled up and purred. Mother came in with his breakfast tray. As she put it on the bed Tim asked, "How did Dr. Still learn to be a doctor?"

"He had made friends with some Indian children who lived near him. Sometimes he went into the woods with them while their mothers gathered roots and herbs to dry or pound into medicine. He learned the names of these different plants. The Indian women told him which ones were good for a fever, and which ones would cure a stomach-ache or a headache."

"Can you really get rid of a stomach-ache or a fever by eating herbs or roots?"

"If you know which ones," Mother said. "Dr. Still studied about them the way other medicines were studied in medical school. And that reminds me, Tim. It's time for a spoonful of your medicine."

Tim didn't like the taste, but if Dr. Still said it would make him better he'd take it.

"Please tell me the rest of the story," he said wrinkling up his nose as he swallowed it.

"Well Tim, one day when James was several years older than you, his father bound him out to a farmer for three years."

"What does that mean?"

"That means that for three years he would live with the farmer and do any work he was told to do. For this his father would get $100 and James would go to school one month in every year. At the end of this time James would get ten dollars and a new suit of clothes.

"Can you imagine, Tim, a big boy many years older than you and your friends coming into your class at school and not knowing how to write, or do arithmetic, and only able to read a few easy words that his mother had taught him at home?"

"Golly, no."

"Well that was how James entered school. But he learned quickly and studied every minute he wasn't working in the fields. He had no boys or girls his age to be friends with. No one to talk to about his plans to be a doctor."

"No friends!" Tim said. "I guess I'm lucky to have so many."

"When he was eighteen and released from his three years with the farmer, he put on his new suit, and with the ten dollars in his pocket he walked all the way to Philadelphia. There he got a job in a glue factory. With the money he earned he bought books. Many of them were about roots and herbs. They told more about preparing them for medicines.

"After several years at this factory he had saved enough money to go back to New Jersey. He bought some land right on the edge of the Pine Barrens and built a little house. Then he gathered roots and herbs and began to make medicines from them. These he sold to druggists in Philadelphia.

"People around here soon learned that he could cure many of their illnesses. They began to call him 'Dr. Still.'"

"Didn't he ever go to medical school?" Tim asked.

"No," said his mother. "But he has probably cured more people than many of the doctors who have taken care of patients in the cities. He uses the medicine that nature gives us, along with good common sense."

Mother went over to the window and looked out across the lake of brown cedar water where Tim liked to swim. "You know, Tim, the doctor who came down here from the city to see you said he couldn't make you well. He didn't believe that you would ever be able to walk, or run, or swim again. That was when we called Dr. Still. We should have called him in the very beginning."

She went back to the bed. Tim had fallen asleep.

"That's good," she said as she took the tray with its empty dish and glass from the bed. "Sleep is good medicine too."

She felt her son's cool cheeks that had been hot with fever for so many days. "Oh Timmy, we're so thankful that Dr. Still made you well. He *is* a great man," she whispered.

The Last Princess:
Indian Ann

"Are you awake, Elizabeth?" Jonathan whispered putting his chubby hand on his sister's shoulder and gently shaking her.

"Mmmm," she said as she uncurled and stretched out in the big four-poster bed.

She and Jonathan had slept well after the long ride yesterday from Philadelphia to Grandmother's farm in Tabernacle. For much of the way they had been the only two passengers on the stagecoach and Elizabeth hadn't felt too brave.

"You're ten years old now, Elizabeth. You can take care of your little brother," Mother had said. "I'll come for you next week if Aunt Rachel is well enough and doesn't need me any longer."

The trip had been long and hot. Elizabeth had gotten tired of making up stories to keep Jonathan amused. They were both glad when the stagecoach arrived at the crossroads and they saw Grandmother waiting for them with Old Clay hitched to the buckboard. Glad too, to tumble into bed after the good supper of rabbit stew and Grandmother's fresh baked bread.

Now, even after a long night's sleep it was hard for Elizabeth to waken.

"Elizabeth, are you still asleep?" the little boy asked impatiently, shaking her again.

"How could I be when you're asking me questions?" she said dreamily.

She stretched once more, then slowly slipped out of bed. Jonathan was already dressed. It didn't take her long to put on her clothes and follow him downstairs to the big roomy kitchen. Grandmother had already prepared their breakfast and had put a little tin pail beside each bowl of mush.

"I though you might like to gather huckleberries down by the clearing this morning," she said. "If you fill these pails we'll have huckleberry buckle for supper."

"Yum," said Elizabeth. "With thick cream on it?"

"If you would like it that way."

"Will we see Indians?" Jonathan asked.

"No, child," Grandmother said. "There are very few Indians in this part of New Jersey any more. They left a long time ago."

"I'm glad. I'd be scared if I saw one," the little boy said.

"Oh no, Jonathan. The Indians who lived here were very friendly."

"Well I'd *still* be scared."

"Well *I'd* like to see a real Indian," Elizabeth said as she picked up the two pails. "Come on, scaredy cat," and she ran down the steps and skipped along the path edged with tall pine trees. Jonathan followed close behind her.

"Don't stay too long," called Grandmother.

The path ended in a large open space where thick huckleberry bushes grew in great clumps. Each branch was heavy with clusters of the tart sweet fruit.

The children put their pails on the ground and started to pick, eating almost as many berries as they dropped into the little buckets. Bees buzzed around them looking for any late blossoms. A large orange butterfly fluttered by. They chased it. The butterfly headed for a daisy field beyond the clearing.

"Let's gather some flowers for Grandmother," Elizabeth said. "Leave your bucket here."

It wasn't long before their arms were full.

"I can't hold any more," Jonathan said. "I'm going home."

"We have to pick the rest of our berries first," said his sister.

They put their daisies in the shade by the path and went back to finish their task, when Jonathan let out a cry.

"Look, Elizabeth. Indians!"

Elizabeth turned around. Sure enough, silently watching them through the bushes was an Indian smoking a long-stemmed clay pipe. The Indian's jet black hair was parted in the middle and braided into two thick braids. A beaded headband circled the high forehead, and the blackest eyes she'd ever seen looked down on Elizabeth. The rest of the Indian was hidden by the leafy branches.

Their eyes met for a brief moment. Jonathan had dropped his pail of berries and was racing across the clearing to the path.

"Wait!" Elizabeth called, picking up the two buckets and darting after him, berries spilling all along the way. Breathlessly they got to the porch steps at the same time.

"Grandmother! Grandmother!" Jonathan shouted. "There are Indians—lots of them down in the huckleberry patch."

Grandmother hurried downstairs.

"They're smoking pipes and they're all painted. . ."

"No, there aren't lots of Indians," Elizabeth interrupted, panting. "I think there is only one Indian."

"No, no," Jonathan said, "there are lots of them. They must be warriors."

"Now just a minute," Grandmother smiled. "Are you sure it is an *Indian* at all?"

"Oh yes, it really *is*," Elizabeth said. "He has black hair plaited in two braids. He's smoking a long pipe."

"How is the Indian dressed, Elizabeth?"

"He was behind the bushes and we couldn't see anything but his head."

"And was there a blue and white band around the Indian's head?"

"Yes, Grandmother. Yes, there was."

"Well I'll tell you about that Indian. First of all he isn't a warrior. He isn't a man. The person you saw is a real Indian princess."

"A princess!" the children both gasped.

"Yes," said Grandmother. "Princess Indian Ann, the daughter of Lasha Tamar, the last chief of the Brotherton Indians who lived close by."

"But he—she was smoking a pipe," Jonathan said.

"Yes, many Indian women smoke pipes."

"Tell us about her," Elizabeth begged.

"The Indians who belonged to Chief Tamar's tribe were very unhappy. Although they were always friendly with the white man, they didn't want to adopt his ways. They didn't want to work in the iron foundries and paper mills that were being built around here. They didn't want to live in houses the way the white man was living. So after a council meeting one day, Chief Tamar led a wagon train of about eighty-five of his people— nearly all that were left of his tribe—to join the Oneida Indians in New York.

"But after a few years the chief longed for his native state. He loved the forests with the sweet smell of cedar and pine. He loved the deer and the rabbits, the possum and raccoon that lived here. He loved the sandy soil where the wild huckle- berries and cranberries grow. So he left his tribe and he and his wife came back to New Jersey. It was here that his little princess, Indian Ann, was born. The chief was very sad that the little girl wouldn't know the ways of his people, but as she grew older he taught her to weave the most beauti- ful baskets."

"Is she still a princess?" Jonathan asked.

"She will always be a princess," Grandmother said. "But now all the Indian land is gone. Chief Tamar died many years ago. Indian Ann doesn't have much money. She doesn't even have a deer-skin teepee. Instead she lives in a tiny wooden house a few miles down the road. But she still weaves beautiful baskets, which she sells or trades at farms for bread or vegetables or bacon."

A knock at the door interrupted Grandmother's story. She opened it.

There stood Indian Ann wearing a shapeless blue flowered dress. Long black braids that reached her waist were held in place by a headband of blue and white beads. She had left her clay pipe on the top step of the porch. In one arm she carried a huge bunch of daisies. Over the other arm she had the most beautiful basket woven with a design in blue and green and yellow.

"Good morning, Ann," Grandmother said.

"Good morning, Mrs. Richards. The children left these by path," and she gave Grandmother the flowers that Elizabeth and Jonathan had picked.

"Thank you. I'm so glad you found them. The children must have forgotten them when they finished gathering their berries." As she took them she said, "Children, come here. I want you to meet Indian Ann."

Elizabeth was already at the door. As she looked into the Indian's black eyes she said, "I'm sorry we ran from you. We didn't know. . ."

Indian Ann reached out her rough brown hand and touched Elizabeth's smooth white cheek. Jonathan edged up behind his sister.

"If you stop by tomorrow I'll have some huckleberry buckle for you," Grandmother said.

"Maybe I will," Indian Ann answered. She turned, picked up her pipe and started down the path puffing away, sending little white whiffs of smoke into the clear summer air.

"Grandmother," Jonathan said as he watched her disappear around the bend in the road, "I didn't think I would ever see a real Indian."

Elizabeth put her hand up to her cheek where Ann had touched it. "I didn't think I would ever see a real princess," she said.

A Tea Party at Greenwich

Jamie stood on the wharf watching a ship glide up the Cohansey River. Its sails were full with the brisk December wind. Jamie thought how great it would be to walk the decks of a ship like that, to hear her ropes creak and watch as her bow cut the water.

As it came closer he could read the name GREY-HOUND, painted on the side.

He was surprised when it headed for the wharf. There weren't any crates or barrels piled around to be loaded on a ship, and no flatwagons were lined up in the street to carry any cargo overland.

"Oh well, it's getting late. They'll probably wait till tomorrow to unload," Jamie said aloud.

The captain edged the GREYHOUND close and the sailors dropped anchor. Jamie watched as they uncoiled the thick ropes and tied her securely against the wharf. The gang-plank was lowered and the captain stepped quickly down from the ship, his long black mustache blowing in the breeze. He walked right over to Jamie.

"Do you live around here, lad?" he asked.

"Yes sir."

"I'm Captain Allen and I'm looking for Dan Bowen. Could you tell me where he lives?"

"Yes sir. He's over by Market Square," Jamie answered. "I could take you there if you'd like."

"Fine, fine. A captain always likes an escort."

Jamie had seen dozens of ships tie up here, and

quite often the ship's master would appear on deck. But this was the first time he ever had a chance to talk with a real captain.

"This way," Jamie said. He put his hands in his pockets and swaggered down the street just a half step ahead of the captain.

"What's your name, lad?"

"James, sir. But everyone calls me Jamie."

"Well Jamie, isn't it a bit late for you to be down on the wharf? I'd judge it's almost your dinner time," the captain said.

"Yes sir, " Jamie agreed. "I was going home when I saw the GREYHOUND headed this way. I wanted to see her dock. Some day I'm going to be a captain of a ship like yours," Jamie said.

Captain Allen smiled. "You must like the sea."

"I've never been out to sea, or even on a big ship, but I know I'd like it."

"Do many ships put in here?"

"Yes, sir."

"Do they bring in much tea?"

"Not so much," Jamie said quietly. "Not any more."

"But I thought the people of this country drank a great deal of tea. I heard the ladies had tea parties every day."

"They used to."

"Used to?" asked the captain.

"Oh gosh," Jamie sighed to himself, "here we go talking about tea again!"

Tea was the subject Jamie's father, mother and

big brother Mark discussed every night at supper. From what they said, Jamie understood that England collected a tax on everything she sold to the colonies—including the tea everyone loved to drink. And the colonies couldn't say anything about it. They just *had to pay the tax.* Jamie's parents thought this was unfair, and so did a lot of other people. They called it "taxation without representation." The citizens of Greenwich had angry meetings in the courthouse to try to decide what to do about it.

"So far all they've done about it is talk," thought Jamie a little irritably. Many of the other colonies had refused to buy the tea sent from England. They wouldn't even allow English ships to dock in some harbors.

The captain interrupted Jamie's thoughts. "Have you heard about the Boston Tea Party?" he asked.

"Yes sir. Everyone in Greenwich has heard about it. And after Boston there was a tea burning in Annapolis."

"Oh!" said the captain. "And what did the people of Greenwich think of that?"

"I'm—I'm not sure." Jamie hesitated. He wondered whether his parents and Mark would want him talking to this English captain about the colonists' destroying cargoes of English tea.

"You're not sure?" the captain asked. "But you *are* sure you know where Dan Bowen lives?"

"Oh yes sir. Is Mr. Bowen your friend?"

"In a business way," the captain replied gruffly. "I

think we'll be better friends after tonight. And who knows," he added with a smile, "maybe the ladies of Greenwich will be drinking tea again quite soon."

"You mean you've brought *tea* on the GREY-HOUND? Is *that* her cargo?" Jamie asked with excitement.

"Well, let's say it's a—a surprise cargo."

"A surprise cargo! Does Mr. Bowen know what it is?"

"Yes he knows. He's—say Jamie, why are you asking me all these questions?" the captain grumbled.

Jamie laughed. "That's what my mother always says. I guess I was just born curious, sir. Well, here's Dan Bowen's house."

"Thank you for bringing me here," said the captain. He stood stiffly at attention and saluted. Jamie stepped back and returned the salute as smartly as he knew how.

"Good lad," Captain Allen remarked with a smile. Then he turned, hurried up the steps and rapped on the door with its heavy brass knocker. The door opened and the captain disappeared inside.

Jamie raced down the cobblestone street as fast as he could. It was dark by the time he got home. Father, Mother and Mark had already started supper. Jamie slid into his seat at the table.

"Well, young man," his father scolded, "where have you been?"

"I was showing Captain Allen where Dan Bowen lives. He has a surprise cargo on his ship the GREYHOUND, and do you know what I think it is?"

"What?" asked Mark.

"I think it's tea."

"Tea!" exclaimed Father and Mother at the same time.

Jamie was so excited he found it difficult to eat. But between mouthfuls he spilled out his story, remembering everything the captain had said— every question he had asked.

After the dishes were washed and put in the cupboard Mark said, "I think Jamie and I should walk down to the wharf. Maybe we can find out if the GREYHOUND really brought in any tea."

"Bundle up well. It's gotten very cold since the sun's gone down," Mother said. "And Mark— be careful."

Jamie put on his jacket, wrapped his scarf around his neck and pulled his cap down over his ears. Mark turned up the collar of his heavy cloak, and the two of them walked quickly down Greate Street. The sky was black. There was no sign of the moon tonight. Even the stars seemed farther away than usual, and gave no light to the silent street.

As they came close to the wharf, Jamie reached for Mark's hand. "Look!" he whispered.

There in the dim glow of the ship's lanterns, they saw sailors carrying chests down the gang-plank and stacking them on the wharf.

"Chests of tea!" Mark exclaimed in a low voice. "You were right, Jamie."

Other sailors carried them off the wharf and down the street.

"Come on," Mark said. "We've got to find out

where they're going."

"I bet they're taking them to Dan Bowen's," Jamie said.

They edged their way along in the darkness until they stood across from Bowen's house. In the faint candle light shining through the open cellar doorway they watched the sailors carry the chests down the steps and pile them against the wall. After the last one was put in place, the cellar door was closed. Almost at once the front door opened and a bright beam of light fell on the steps and was reflected in the brass knocker. Captain Allen and Dan Bowen shook hands, the door closed and again everything was inky-black.

The brothers quietly stole home.

"Jamie, you mustn't tell anyone what you saw tonight," Mark said. "Do you understand?"

"Sure I understand. Do you think I'm a baby and don't know anything?" Jamie asked in a hurt voice.

"Of course I don't think you're a baby. But Jamie, this might be the beginning of very serious business, and I don't want you involved," Mark said putting his arm around the young boy's shoulder.

"But what if Father and Mother ask questions?"

"They won't," Mark answered. "Don't worry about that. You know they let us have our secrets."

As soon as they stepped inside their house, Jamie was sent to bed.

"You should have been here an hour ago," Mother scolded gently.

It was a long time before Jamie could fall asleep.

He heard the muted sounds of Mother, Father and Mark talking far into the night, until finally his excitement gave way to exhaustion.

During the night the GREYHOUND slipped down the Cohansey River and in the morning the wharf was empty.

The next few nights were busy for everyone but Jamie. Mark was off with his friends Joel Fithian and Lewis Howell. His father attended meetings of the "Sons of Liberty." His mother and some of the women of Greenwich were organizing the "Daughters of Liberty." Jamie spent his spare time reading, curled up in his favorite wing chair in the alcove of the big kitchen. Sometimes he turned the chair around so that its back was toward the kitchen table. As he read about sailing vessels, he pretended that this corner was the captain's quarters, and he was on his own ship.

One windy night about a week after Captain Allen's visit to Greenwich, Jamie was in the corner reading when there was a knock on the door. Mark answered it. Joel, Lewis, and two other young men entered the house. They took off their cloaks and caps, followed Mark into the kitchen and seated themselves around the table. Mother poured out mugs of hot coffee. Then she left the room, closing the door after her.

"Well, plans are almost complete for our little party on the 22nd," Joel said, not noticing Jamie sitting in his turned-around chair in the corner. "Tonight we'll have to figure out a way to get into

Dan Bowen's cellar. We couldn't possibly enter his house by the front door. And the cellar door is bolted on the inside. If we break it down we'll make so much noise the whole town would hear."

"Somehow," Mark said, "the door will have to be opened from the inside. For a moment today I thought I had a solution when I found one of his cellar windows unlocked. But the opening is so small that none of us could could get through."

"How about the windows upstairs?" someone asked.

"It's too risky," Joel said. "Anyway, Bowen probably has a lock on the door that leads down cellar from the kitchen. No, that wouldn't work."

Jamie could keep quiet no longer. He peered around the back of the chair. "I could slide through his cellar window," he said. "I'm small enough."

All five young men turned startled eyes toward what they had thought was an empty chair in the corner.

"Jamie, I thought you were in bed!" Mark scowled.

"Nobody told me to go," Jamie said. He came over to his brother. "Please let me do it. I know I could."

"No, no, it's too dangerous," Mark said firmly.

"Please!" Jamie pleaded, "I'd be careful."

"It seems to me, Jamie already has a part in this party," Lewis said. "He was the one who told you about the tea in the first place."

"And if we can't get in the cellar we won't even

have a party," one of the others added.

Mark nodded. "You're both right. I guess I didn't realize how much we needed Jamie."

"You mean I can do it then!" the boy exclaimed.

Mark smiled, and Jamie knew the smile meant, "Yes."

His eyes danced with excitement as he listened to their plans. They had already made torches of birch branches with a coating of tar at one end. These were leaning against Joel's woodshed a few miles out of town. Everything else was checked and ready.

Jamie could hardly do any work at school the next day for thinking about the part he would have in the tea party.

December 22nd arrived.

After dinner Mother said that he could ride with Mark to the Fithian place. Mark saddled Rex. He pulled Jamie up behind him and they rode off. Many of Mark's friends were there when they arrived. They all smeared their faces with red, blue and white paint, and dressed in costumes resembling Indian clothes. Jamie didn't recognize himself when he looked in the mirror. Then each one took a torch and rode back to Market Square.

Quietly they slipped from their horses, stacked their torches against a tree and walked noiselessly over to Dan Bowen's. At the back of the house they located the tiny unlocked cellar window and raised it bit by bit. Mark lighted a lantern and held it through the opening.

"Look, Jamie," he whispered. "You see how far you have to drop to the floor? As soon as you're there I'll hand you the lantern. Then you can find your way to the door and unbolt it. You're not afraid?"

"N-o-o, of course not. It's not very far to drop," Jamie said, trying to sound much braver than he felt.

Mark withdrew the lantern. Jamie pulled his head out of the blackness, turned around, then, feet first, he slithered through the opening. And he was in the dark cellar all alone. Mark handed him the lantern. In its flickering light his shadows seemed ten feet tall. They shimmered against the chests of tea. Fearfully he picked his way to the door and put the lantern on the floor. With both hands he pushed against the heavy iron bolt. It slid easily. Then he pulled back the door. It creaked open.

Mark was right outside. "That's great, Jamie," he whispered.

The "Indians" worked quickly hauling out the chests. They carried them to the square, broke them open and dumped the tea on the ground. It made a huge mound.

When the last chest had been emptied, one of the young men lighted a torch from Jamie's lantern. It sputtered, then flared into a bright yellow flame. He touched it to the pile of tea. The tea caught fire. Each "Indian" did the same thing. Soon a blaze lighted up the whole length of Greate

Street. The "Indians" danced around it, whooping and shouting. And the smallest "Indian" made the loudest noise of all.

The townspeople came to the square to see what was going on, and they too danced around the bonfire.

Then, all of a sudden the conspirators mounted their horses and galloped away. Back at Joel's house they washed their faces and changed into their own clothes, and Mark and Jamie rode home. The bonfire had died out. Nothing was left of the tea but ashes.

It had been a long, exciting night—and for Jamie, a little scary.

"You're a brave boy. I'm proud of you," Mark said as they stopped in front of the house. He eased his brother down from the saddle. "I'll see you inside as soon as I've put Rex in the stable."

Jamie wished he could tell his father and mother what they had done, but Mark said not to mention it.

As Jamie walked into the living room Mother looked up from her mending and said, "We certainly had some excitement after you left to visit the Fithians! There must have been twenty-five Indians who rode up Greate Street and set fire to a mound of tea in Market Square. Everyone in town came out to see it. What a pity you weren't here. But it's late, Jamie," she said, standing up. "We'll tell you all about it in the morning. You had better go to bed now." She kissed him good night.

"Before you go, Son," his father said putting his

arm around Jamie's shoulder, "I want you to know that I think we have some very brave young men—and boys—here in Greenwich. I don't always approve of the way they do things, but I'm sure that sparks from tonight's fire will help light other torches of liberty for a new nation." He kissed his son's cheek. "Now off with you."

As he started toward the stairs Mother said, "Jamie, there's a smudge of something that looks like blue paint above your left eyebrow. Better wash it off before you go to bed." And she winked at him.

The Night Simon Saw the Jersey Devil

"Now I expect you to be nice to Cousin Simon," Mother said to the twins as she put her foot on the wagon step and pulled herself up to the seat beside Father. "No more of this tripping and hitting one another. Behave like the eleven-year-olds that you are."

"But Simon always starts it," Sara said.

"And he's bigger than we are," added Mathew.

"Enough of that," boomed Father's voice from the other side of the wagon. "We're counting on all three of you to behave. And be sure to keep the fire burning in the fireplace. We'll be home from the meeting before midnight." He gave the reins a little flip and Old Red started the wagon on its way.

Cousin Simon was perched on the rail fence. Rolling the piece of straw he was chewing to the side of his mouth, he called "I'll take care of them, Aunt."

Sara frowned. "We don't need to be taken care of," she said under her breath. "I'll be glad when he goes back home."

Six days had been a long time to be teased and poked and tripped. Even Shep, the gentlest dog in the world, growled when Simon came near, and the cats both scurried under the bed so they wouldn't have their tails pulled.

Simon hopped off the rail fence and started up the path to the farmhouse. The twins watched the wagon disappear down the road. The rays of the setting sun were beginning to filter through the pine trees. In the east a sliver of moon was just visible through gauzy clouds.

"A new moon," Sara said. "I'm going to make a wish." She closed her eyes tight. "I wish that Simon goes back to Philadelphia sooner than we thought he would."

At the door Simon turned. "Let's go down to the pond and catch frogs," he called back.

"You won't be able to see them," Mathew said. "By the time you get there it will be dark."

"Besides you don't let them go after you catch them. You only hurt them," Sara said.

"That sounds just like a girl," Simon sneered. "Well, what do you want to do?"

"Let's go in and get some gingerbread."

"Sounds good," Mathew said.

"I'll force some," Simon grumbled as he went in and stretched out on the floor in front of the fireplace.

It was almost dark now. Mathew lighted the oil lamp. Sara cut the gingerbread, poured three glasses of milk and brought it all from the kitchen. She and Mathew sat on the floor beside Simon. Shep snuggled between them. Simon threw the straw he had been chewing into the fire and watched it shrivel and burn. Then he took a huge swallow of milk. He spit it out and screwed up his face.

"This milk's sour," he whined.

Sara and Mathew tasted theirs. It surely was sour.

"Why did Aunt leave sour milk for us to drink?" Simon set his glass down with a bang. Drops bounced out on the floor.

"Mother didn't know it was sour," Sara said.

"It probably wasn't when she set it out. Maybe the Jersey Devil did it," Mathew said. "That's the kind of trick he plays."

"What's the Jersey Devil?" Simon asked.

"Haven't you ever heard of him? He travels all through the Pine Barrens."

Simon shook his head.

"He's a monster that goes around playing all kinds of pranks on people. Making milk sour is one of his favorites. Sometimes he even makes the cows dry so they don't give milk. He pulls up corn stalks and tramples the other vegetables in the fields," Mathew said.

Simon snickered. He took a big bite of gingerbread, and while his mouth was still full he said, "I don't believe you. I don't think there's any Jersey Devil."

"Well you better believe us," Sara said. "He was born at Leeds Point, not very far from here. His mother already had twelve children. She didn't know what she would do with any more. When the thirteenth child was born she was so upset she said, "I wish you'd fly away." When she laid him in the cradle he started to change from a cute little baby into an ugly monster. His body became long and skinny and he had a big forked tail. His hands and feet became hoofs. His face changed to look like a horse. And at his shoulders huge bat wings began to grow. He flapped them a few times and then flew right up the chimney."

Mathew looked over to where the smoke was slowly curling up *their* chimney. Simon looked too. Then he looked around the room.

"Does he ever come into people's houses?" he asked.

"He usually just roams around outside peeking in windows. You can tell when it's the Jersey Devil though, because his green eyes glow in the dark."

"Wheew!" breathed Simon. "Did you ever see him?"

"No. But lots of people say they have. He often comes when boys and girls don't behave."

"They say he's so strong he can blow the tops right off trees," Sara said.

Outside the wind began to howl. It whistled down the chimney and blew a little puff of smoke into the room. Then they heard a mournful wail way off in the woods. It got louder. The wail turned into a screech as it came closer. In the distance several dogs barked. Shep's ears stood up in sharp points and he growled deep down in his throat.

They heard a squeak. Then a bang. The squeak again. Another bang!

"Yep," said Mathew, "it must be the Jersey Devil. He's prowling around tonight. Maybe he's looking for Simon."

"Oh no," said Simon with a shiver, putting his hands over his eyes.

Mathew looked at Sara and winked.

"I wonder if the pirate ghost is with him?" Sara said.

"Pirate ghost?" Simon whispered, taking his hands from his eyes.

"Yes," said Mathew. "When Captain Kidd buried his treasure down by Barnegat Bay, he made one of his pirates stay there to guard it. The pirate drowned one day and the Jersey Devil became friends with his ghost. The two of them often travel through the Barrens together."

A scratching at the window interrupted Mathew's story. The three children looked to see what it was. Through the panes glowed two big green eyes.

"It *is* the Jersey Devil!" cried Simon. "He looks just like you said," and he buried his head in his lap, clasping his hands behind his neck.

Shep whined and put his head on his paws. The fire sputtered.

"We need more wood or the fire will go out. Look, it's our last log and Father told us to be sure to keep it going," Sara said. "Simon, today was your turn to bring in wood, and you didn't do it. You better go out to the woodpile and get an armful."

"I'm not going outside. The Jersey Devil is still there." He lifted his head and squinted at the window. The green eyes were no longer peering at him.

"You said you didn't believe there was any Jersey Devil."

"That was before I saw him looking in the window."

"But he isn't looking at us now. The fire is going out. We've got to keep it burning. And Simon, you've got to get the wood."

"Please, please, I don't want to go out there. Mathew, won't you and Sara get it tonight? You're both so brave. Take Shep with you. He'll protect you, and he wouldn't go with me. Tomorrow I'll bring in a whole stack of wood. I'll bring it in the next *two* days."

"Well I don't know. It's not our responsibility. It's yours," Mathew said.

"I'll bring it in *three* days," Simon said.

"If we get it tonight will you promise not to tease and trip us any more?" Sara asked.

"Yes, I promise."

"And you won't tease Shep either?"

"I promise."

"Or pull the cats' tails?"

"No. No."

"And you won't hurt the frogs when you catch them?"

"No, I won't. I'll let them hop right back in the pond."

"Suppose *we* meet the Jersey Devil," Mathew said. "Suppose he carries one of *us* off with him."

"Oh but he won't. There'll be two of you—and Shep. I'm sure he wouldn't hurt you."

"If you come there'll be three of us—and Shep."

"Please let me stay here," Simon pleaded.

"Do you think we should get the wood for him just this one time?" Mathew asked.

"Yes, this one time," Sara said, "if you think he'll really keep all his promises."

"I will. I will," Simon said.

When the twins were outside they started to laugh. They laughed until their sides hurt. Shep pranced around them making happy little yips. By now the wind had died down. Way off in the distance they again heard the mournful wail as screech owls called to each other. They went around to the side of the house. There on the wide windowsill one of the cats was curled up asleep, its front paws doubled under its chin.

"Kitty, your eyes shone like two green lanterns when you looked in the window at us. You sure scared Simon. I don't think he'll pull your tail any more." Sara scratched his ears, and the cat purred loudly. Then he stretched out his full length and went to sleep again on the sill.

The twins went to the woodshed. "I'm glad Father didn't know I forgot to put oil on these hinges," Mathew said. "But wasn't tonight the best night to have this door squeak and bang?" They gathered as much wood as their arms would hold. Mathew closed and latched the woodshed door. "I think we scared Simon enough for one night."

Shep followed the children into the house.

Simon was still hunched up by the dying fire, his head buried in his lap and his hands over his ears. He looked up as Mathew put a log on the fire and fanned the flame to get it burning bright again.

"Did you see him? Did you see the Jersey Devil?" Simon asked.

"No," said Mathew trying not to laugh.

"I heard him while you were out there. He must have been flying away."

"He must have been," Mathew said. "Tomorrow we'll look for his footprints. He usually leaves them under the window when he's been peeping into the house."

"I don't want to see his footprints," Simon said. "I just want to go home. Tomorrow I'm going to ask Uncle to put me on the stagecoach to Philadelphia. I like it better where there isn't any Jersey Devil to scare the wits out of me and make the milk go sour. I don't like to bring in firewood and stack it. And I don't think it's much fun catching frogs."

Mathew looked at Sara and winked.

"I'm sure glad I saw that new moon and made a wish on it," Sara said to herself.

Blackbeard the Pirate

"We'll take the path through the woods and sleep down by the river," Ben said. "Remember the cove with the sandy beach, Rob?"

"Sure I remember. The place we went swimming last year."

"That's the one."

"How far is it?" Derik asked.

"Now listen, Derik, if you're going to get tired before we start you better stay home," Rob said.

The two older boys tramped through the woods every time Rob came down from Philadelphia to visit. This year Mother said that, as long as they were twelve years old, they were surely responsible enough to look after Derik. He wanted so much to go with them.

"I won't get tired, I promise," the little boy said. "I only wanted to know how far it is."

"Well it's a pretty long way, Small Portion. Sure you can make it?" Ben asked.

"I'm sure."

The sun was sliding lazily toward the horizon when they left the house.

"Don't forget to bring back those blankets," Mother called as the boys started down the path to the woods.

It was so quiet walking through the forest. The pines smelled good and the cool breezes blowing through them made a sound just like rain when it fell on the shingled roof of the farmhouse. Sometimes when Ben awakened in the middle of the night he couldn't tell whether he heard rain or wind blowing through the trees.

He knew the path to the river with his eyes closed. He often walked to the little cove all alone. It was his favorite thinking place. Propped up against a tree he would look down the river, wondering what it was like in those far-off places where sailing vessels took on their cargo of sugar or molasses.

They had walked quite a distance when Ben put his arm across Derik's shoulder. "Stand still," he whispered.

The boys froze. In a few seconds four white-tailed deer leaped across the path in front of them. They watched them disappear into the thicket.

"How could you tell they were coming, Ben?" Rob asked.

"Oh, I don't know. I just could, that's all."

"Ben knows everything about the woods," Derik said. He took his big brother's hand.

"Getting tired, Small Portion?" Ben asked.

"A little," Derik confessed.

"We're almost there now."

As the forest began to grow darker it seemed to waken with all kinds of strange noises. Undergrowth stirred as a possum or raccoon started his evening prowl. Overhead echoed the eerie sound of night hawks calling to one another. Then all of a sudden the path turned sharply, opening out on a small cove. And there before them lay the Maurice

River, smooth and golden in the rays of the setting sun. A wide sandy beach separated the river from the tall pines that protected the cove. Their huge branches drooped close to the ground, making great circles around their trunks.

Ben picked out his favorite tree. "Let's sleep here," he said.

They pushed aside the low branches. It was large and roomy in the center. There was plenty of space to stretch out and sleep. Needles had fallen year after year covering the ground with a thick soft carpet, just as comfortable as Ben's corn-husk mattress at home.

By now the sun had dropped from sight.

"We better hurry if we're going to take a swim," Rob said.

"I'm too tired," Derik said. "I'll watch you." He curled up in his blanket and propped himself against the tree trunk.

Ben and Rob quickly undressed. Tossing their clothes over at Derik they raced to the water.

At first it felt comfortably warm, but in a short while a chill breeze sprang up. It was growing dark rapidly.

"Better go dry off," Ben said.

They dressed, wrapped up in their blankets and stretched out on the soft ground. By now the river looked like a sheet of black glass cut in half by a path of silver made by the moon as it rose higher in the sky. Somewhere in the distance an owl hooted, and almost overhead it was answered by a loud, "Whoo, whoo."

Derik reached out for Ben.

"You're not scared, are you, Small Portion?"

"No," the little boy answered shakily. "I just wanted to be sure you were there."

They were all quiet for a while. Then Ben asked, "Did you know that Blackbeard the pirate used to sail up this river? He even buried treasure on one of the beaches around here. Did you know that, Derik?"

There was no answer.

"Did you know that, Rob?"

There was still no answer.

"What company," Ben said. "Both of them are asleep!"

He wrapped his blanket closer about him and sat with his back against the tree trunk, watching the moon as it got higher and higher. He wished he had his book with him—the one Father had bought in Philadelphia. He could read it out there on the beach; the moon was bright enough.

As he looked out over the river a mist seemed to

rise. Through the shadows a sailing vessel slowly moved up the quiet water. Ben watched it grow larger and larger. Its great sails were full, even though there didn't seem to be much breeze. When it reached the spot opposite the cove it dropped anchor. Suddenly the mist dispersed, and in the light of the full moon Ben could clearly see in large white letters on the side of the ship, QUEEN ANNE'S REVENGE.

"Blackbeard's pirate ship!" Ben breathed.

A longboat was lowered into the river. Several men climbed down a rope ladder into it. Another longboat was lowered and more men followed.

Ben heard the slow swish, swish, swish, as the oars broke the water. Closer and closer they rowed. When they reached the beach the men all piled over the side and nosed the crafts up on the sand. A big black dog jumped out and ran up and down the beach. Several men lifted a chest from the first boat and carried it to the edge of the clearing. They put it in the shadows and went back to get another chest. And another. One of the men heaved a sack up on his shoulder, about the size of the one Ben's father put potatoes in after they dug them from the field. He carried it over and leaned it against the chests.

"Now heave to and find some wood, Mateys," boomed the raucous voice of the biggest pirate.

"That must be Blackbeard," Ben whispered to himself.

Moonlight casting a shadow behind the pirate made him look ten feet tall.

"We'll start a fire and have some rum," he bellowed.

The pirates searched through the woods for sticks and fallen branches. They came so close to the boys that Ben thought they would hear his heart beating. He scarcely dared breathe. Then the big black dog found them. He stood there in the moonlight and growled down deep in his throat. The short hair on his back stood up straight, from his neck to his tail. Ben watched him standing where the lowest branches of the tree touched the ground, concealing the three boys.

"What if he barks?" Ben thought.

The enormous creature padded in through the branches and sniffed around Ben. Then he sniffed around the two sleeping boys. No one moved. Finally the dog relaxed. Apparently satisfied that there was no danger here, it ran back to the pirates.

Ben breathed a deep "Wheew!"

The fire had started and the dry logs sent sparks high into the sky. In its light Ben watched the motley crew.

Blackbeard was the tallest. Below his battered tricorn his eyes peered out of a face covered with a gigantic black beard. His hair was plaited in two braids and reached below his shoulders. Ben had heard that when he was raiding another ship, he put lighted tapers in the ends of the braids to make him look more ferocious. His coat, knee breeches and stockings were all black. Hanging from his shoulder was a wide band strung with an arsenal of pistols. Two cutlasses tucked in his belt gleamed in the firelight.

Most of the pirates wore colored kerchiefs around their heads, and large silver earrings hung from their ears.

The black dog singled out one of the crew and stretched out on the sand beside him.

Blackbeard's voice boomed through the sound of the crackling fire, "Bring me a bottle of rum!"

Ben heard an owl in the distance call "Whoo?"

"You over there," Blackbeard bellowed. He pulled a cutlass from his belt and pointed to the pirate with a patch over his eye. "Get the sack."

The pirate pulled the sack to the fire, reached in and handed a bottle to Blackbeard. He took a few gulps then threw back his head and laughed. "Well, Mateys," he said, "heave to. Rum for all."

The pirates grabbed their bottles, and as they drank they began to sing and laugh and shout at each other.

The noise and carousing went on until the moon was high in the sky. The bonfire began to die out. Then, just as suddenly as the celebration started, Blackbeard stopped it. He pulled one of the pistols from his belt and, brandishing it in the firelight, he pointed it at the pirate with the patch.

"You," he shouted. "Get the shovels and start digging over there under that tree."

The pirate brought as many shovels as he could carry from the longboat.

"You too, Mateys. All of you—dig."

They worked furiously making a pit that grew wider and deeper, until those working it it were almost hidden from sight. When Blackbeard thought it was the right size they lowered the chests down into it.

"Now heave to and fill it up good," he thundered. "We've got to get downriver before sun-up."

The chests were covered, the hole filled and the ground tamped down. The pirates and the black dog climbed back in their longboats. They pushed off. Except for the swish, swish, swish of oars, there wasn't a sound as they rowed back to the QUEEN ANNE'S REVENGE. A mist had again risen, enveloping the ship so that Ben could hardly tell when it started to slip away.

The sky was getting brighter. Not the silver brightness of moonlight, but the rosy lavender of a new day dawning.

Ben rubbed his eyes. The other boys were still asleep. He unwrapped himself from his blanket and went down to the water's edge. QUEEN ANNE'S REVENGE had sailed out of sight. He walked over to the spot where the pirates had buried the chests. There was no sign of the ground having been disturbed. It was packed just as firm as it was under the tree where Derik and Rob were sleeping, and covered with the same thick carpet of pine needles. He walked back to the water's edge. There wasn't a mark in the soft sand where the boats had been pulled up—and not a footprint.

Had the tide come in that quickly to cover up the marks in the sand?

Ben was puzzled.

He walked to the side of the cove. There on the very spot where the pirates had built their bonfire was a large patch of warm white ashes. And a short distance away a dozen or more bottles were piled on a sack marked, "Jamaica Rum."

Ben scratched his head. A frown wrinkled his forehead.

"I wonder if Rob and Derik will believe it when I tell them what I saw," he said aloud.

Afterword

These stories could all be true.

The Pine Barrens cover a part of New Jersey 80 miles long and 30 miles wide. The soil is very sandy and the lakes and streams are brown cedar water. Here you will find trees that never grow any taller than you are, and plants that eat insects. Here are ghost towns that were once happy villages like Tabernacle, where Elizabeth's grandmother lived.

Many years ago, pirates sailed up and down the rivers that run through the Pine Barrens and empty into bays along the Atlantic coast. It is quite possible that Blackbeard buried his chests of gold and silver on some of the sandy beaches, although not one of these treasures has ever been found.

This is where the Lenape Indians lived. It was the home of Indian Ann, the daughter of the last chief of the Brotherton Reservation.

Here in the Barrens, James Still, a black boy, grew up and decided to become a doctor. The story Tim's mother told about Dr. Still is all true.

Here, too, a little Italian prince, Constantino di Ruspoli, was born. It is very possible that he could have made friends with an Indian boy.

And this is the home of the Jersey Devil. Some people say that he still roams the Barrens. But I don't know anyone who has *really* seen him.

The medicine shows no longer travel through the Pines. Perhaps this is good, because the medi-

cine men weren't always truthful about the mix-
tures they sold. But some, like Keziah's pa, made a
syrup of herbs and roots which really made people
feel better.

Smithville is now a historic site. You may visit
Hezekiah B. Smith's mansion and some of the
workers' homes like the one where Jody lived.
There is no longer a Smithville Silver Cornet
Band, or a moose named February, but there were
in the 1880's. And the factory where Jody's pa
worked is still operating, making woodworking
machines.

Although Greenwich isn't located in the Pine
Barrens, it is quite close to them. The Tea Party
was such an important event in New Jersey history
that I wanted to include a story about it in this
book. As I started to write, I decided that a boy like
Jamie could have been part of it all.

Bibliography

Bisbee, Henry H. *Signposts*, Alexia Press, 1971.

Burlington County Cultural and Heritage Commission, *The Historic County of Burlington*, 1973.

————, *A Brief History of Smithville*, 1976.

McCloy, James F. and Miller, Ray, Jr. *The Jersey Devil*, The Middle Atlantic Press, 1976.

McMahon, William. *South Jersey Towns*, Rutgers University Press, 1973.

McPhee, John. *The Pine Barrens*, Farrar, Straus & Giroux, 1967.

Pierce, Arthur D. *Smugglers' Woods*, Rutgers University Press, 1960.

Still, James. *Early Recollections*, Medford Historical Society, 1971.